LOMELINO'S

ICE CREAM

LOMELINO'S
ICE CREAM

79 | Ice Creams, Sorbets, and Frozen
     | Treats to Make Any Day Sweet

LINDA LOMELINO

ROOST
BOOKS

Boston & London

2015

CONTENTS

FACT: Ice cream is one of the best treats in life. It's good anytime, anyplace, any season. It makes the everyday more luxurious and is perfect for children's parties and special desserts. Every flavor has an occasion, but why limit yourself? Why *not* serve an affogato when it's cold outside? Or a refreshing watermelon sorbet on a hot summer day? And who would refuse a scoop of dulce de leche and chocolate semifreddo any time of year?

Another fact: The best ice cream is homemade ice cream. I can almost guarantee that once you discover how easy and wonderful it is to make yourself, you'll never buy it from a store again.

Linda Lomelino

EVERYTHING YOU NEED TO KNOW
ABOUT MAKING ICE CREAM

TYPES OF ICE CREAM

ICE CREAM is dairy based and usually made with heavy cream, milk, and egg yolks, but it might even contain cream cheese or condensed milk, depending on the recipe or desired texture.

SORBET is a refreshing frozen treat with many variations. It is usually made with pureed fruit and added sweetener. Because it is dairy-free, it's safe for anyone with milk allergies or lactose intolerance.

SHERBET is a blend of sorbet and cream-based ice cream. Its flavor profile is more like sorbet—smooth, light, and fruity—even with added milk or cream.

SEMIFREDDO, or "half frozen," is an Italian-style frozen dessert. The perk of this dessert: you do not need an ice cream machine to make it.

METHODS FOR MAKING ICE CREAM

When I want rich and creamy ice cream, I start with a base of milk or cream and egg yolks that has been heated and thickened into a custard on the stove top. A good way to test the thickness of the custard is to dip a spoon into it. When you lift the spoon from the custard, it should be coated and the custard should not pour off immediately.

A quick-and-easy style of making ice cream involves blending the core ingredients without heat. This method also produces delicious ice cream, just a touch less luxurious. This is how I make sorbet, sherbet, and shortcut variations of some ice creams (such as the Quick Vanilla and Extra-Rich Chocolate ice cream recipes on pages 13 and 19).

KITCHEN TOOLS

ICE CREAM MACHINE. An ice cream machine is a worthwhile investment—although you can make tasty ice cream without one. It speeds up the freezing process, but more important, it incorporates air into the ice cream while it freezes so the mixture will be creamy and soft. Note that you have to freeze the machine's bowl for about twenty-four hours before you start making the ice cream. *Shortcut:* If you have room in your freezer, just store the bowl there. Before buying an ice cream machine, make sure that the bowl fits in your freezer.

Depending on your model of ice cream machine, it usually takes approximately twenty to fifty minutes for ice cream to freeze to the right consistency. If you want your ice cream very soft, you can serve it directly from the machine. I prefer to let ice cream set another two to three hours in the freezer so it will be easier to scoop.

SAUCEPAN. Needed for making the ice cream base in most recipes.

MEASURING CUP AND SPOONS. A measuring spoon set includes one-quarter and one-half teaspoons and a teaspoon and a tablespoon. Measuring cups are usually marked in portions of a cup, including one-quarter, one-third, one-half, two-thirds, and a full cup as well as in milliliters. All ingredients in my recipes are measured out with these basic units.

SIEVE. A sieve helps separate out bits of cooked egg and seeds from fruit from your ice cream mixture.

SPATULA. Use a spatula to scrape out ice cream or to combine ingredients. Choose one that is heat resistant, especially when cooking custards.

BOWLS. You might need several bowls when you make ice cream. It is helpful to have one that is large enough to set a sieve on as you pour custard or another mixture. When chilling ice cream, a stainless steel bowl cools more quickly.

INGREDIENTS

EGGS. I prefer large eggs for making ice cream. Many recipes call for only egg yolks. Reserve any leftover egg whites for meringues or semifreddo.

MILK. Use whole milk with 3 percent fat. The lower the fat content, the higher the water content and the icier the ice cream will be.

CREAM. Use cream with a fat content of 36 to 40 percent for the best results.

FRUIT AND BERRIES. It is best to use fruits and berries in season. They should be ripe and soft to best bring out their natural flavors. If you are making a fruit-based ice cream with unripe fruit, you may need to add more sugar to compensate. If the fruit or berries you want are out of season, use frozen fruit or berries instead. Fruit is frozen at the peak of its season (and peak freshness), so the flavor will be comparable to that of fresh-picked fruit.

VANILLA. You can use whole vanilla beans, vanilla powder, vanilla sugar, and vanilla extract in these recipes. Vanilla powder is vanilla bean in powdered form. Vanilla sugar is confectioners' sugar flavored with vanilla beans and natural vanilla flavor derived from spruce wood (lignin). Vanilla extract is made with vanilla beans steeped in alcohol.

LIQUEUR. A few teaspoons of liqueur in ice cream keeps it from freezing too hard, decreases the number of ice crystals, and makes the ice cream unbelievably creamy and soft. Best of all, the ice cream thaws faster once you remove it from the freezer. Plus, liqueur adds a layer of flavor.

PREPARING THE ICE CREAM

First, make sure that the bowl for the ice cream machine has been in the freezer long enough (often up to twenty-four hours) and is ready to use.

Ingredients such as toasted nuts should be prepared ahead of time to cool. Put them in a bowl and refrigerate them, covered, for at least an hour.

Freeze the pan or bowl (if you are using an ice cream machine) that you want to store the ice cream in for at least thirty minutes ahead of time. The ice cream just taken out of a frozen machine bowl will melt in a room-temperature pan or bowl.

If the ice cream recipe calls for cooking a custard base, make the base the evening before you plan to make the ice cream. Cover the bowl with plastic wrap and refrigerate it overnight. By morning, the mixture will be ready for the ice cream machine. This method allows the flavor to "ripen," and the result will be extra creamy.

The mixture is ready to be transferred to the ice cream machine when it is the consistency of soft-serve ice cream: smooth, creamy, not quite pourable, and it holds its shape well. Ice cream is considered set (and "ready" to eat) after it has been in the freezer for two to three hours.

MAKING ICE CREAM WITHOUT A MACHINE

It is very easy to make ice cream without an ice cream machine, but the consistency won't be exactly the same. The biggest challenge of making sorbet without a machine is that it easily becomes icy.

Extra-Rich Chocolate Ice Cream (see page **19**) will be just as delicious without a machine. Ice cream cakes (see pages **78–91**) and semifreddo (see pages **55–57**) are made without a machine.

BASIC INSTRUCTIONS. Follow the recipe instructions, and chill the bowl with the custard/ice cream base either in an ice bath or in the refrigerator until the mixture is completely cold. Next, place the bowl in the freezer and stir or whisk the ice cream three to four times as it freezes, about once per hour, using either a large spoon or an electric mixer. This process reduces the ice crystals as much as possible. After three to four hours, the ice cream should be ready to serve.

ICE CREAM

QUICK VANILLA ICE CREAM

Ice cream doesn't get easier than this—a truly simple recipe and unbelievably good vanilla ice cream. Need more inspiration? Try it with some of the extras suggested on page 17.

MAKES 1 PINT

²/₃ cup milk
6 tablespoons granulated sugar
1 cup heavy cream
¹/₂ teaspoon vanilla powder
1 teaspoon vanilla extract or vodka (optional)

1. Whisk the milk and sugar together in a bowl until the sugar is dissolved. Stir in the cream, the vanilla powder, and if desired the vanilla extract or vodka.
2. Process the ingredients in the ice cream machine until ready and then pour the ice cream into a chilled bowl. Freeze 2–3 hours before serving.

EXTRA-RICH VANILLA ICE CREAM

To make this ice cream especially creamy and tasty, add a teaspoon of vanilla extract. If you don't have extract on hand, use a little vodka instead. You can tinker with the flavor by trying one of the extras in the next recipe.

MAKES 2½ CUPS

½ vanilla bean
¾ cup milk
6 tablespoons granulated sugar
pinch of salt
3 large egg yolks
1¼ cups heavy cream
1 teaspoon vanilla extract or vodka (optional)

1. Split the vanilla bean down the center and scrape out the seeds from one half (save the other half for another recipe).
2. Combine the milk, sugar, salt, vanilla seeds, and vanilla bean in a saucepan and heat the mixture until it reaches the boiling point. Remove the pan from the heat and put a lid on it; let the mixture cool on the countertop for 30 minutes.
3. Lightly beat the egg yolks in a small bowl.
4. Reheat the milk mixture and then slowly pour the hot milk over the egg yolks, whisking constantly. Pour the milk/egg mixture back into the saucepan and heat, stirring constantly until the mixture has thickened.
5. Pour the cream into a bowl and set a sieve over the bowl. Strain the heated milk mixture through the sieve and mix it into the cream. Add the vanilla extract or vodka, if desired.

Cover the bowl with plastic wrap and refrigerate, preferably overnight. You can also place the bowl in the freezer for a short while to cool the mixture more quickly.

6. Process the mixture in the ice cream machine until ready and then transfer the ice cream to a chilled bowl. Freeze 2–3 hours before serving.

See page 102 for Cherry Sauce recipe. ⟫→

FLAVORED VANILLA ICE CREAM

Both the Quick and the Extra-Rich Vanilla Ice Cream recipes are perfect bases for adding a variety of flavors. Here are a few suggestions.

STRACCIATELLA

1 recipe vanilla ice cream (see pages **13** and **15**)
3½ oz. dark chocolate (70% cacao) or milk chocolate

1. Make the vanilla ice cream per the instructions. Melt the chocolate in a double boiler or in the microwave. When the ice cream is almost ready, drizzle the melted chocolate in a thin stream directly into the churning ice cream maker. Process a little longer until the ice cream is set.
2. If you aren't using an ice cream machine, drizzle the melted chocolate in a very thin stream over the half-frozen ice cream. As you stir the ice cream occasionally, the chocolate will break into small pieces.

CHOCOLATE-TOFFEE ICE CREAM

1 recipe vanilla ice cream (see pages **13** and **15**)
5¼ oz. chopped Heath Bar (or other chocolate-covered toffee candy)

1. Make the vanilla ice cream per the instructions.
2. When the ice cream is nearly ready, add the chopped toffee candy pieces. Process a little longer until the ice cream is set.

BANANA ICE CREAM

1 recipe vanilla ice cream (see pages **13** and **15**)
3 ripe bananas
1 tablespoon lemon juice

1. Make the vanilla ice cream per the instructions.
2. Before churning the ice cream, mash the bananas with the lemon juice and stir them into the ice cream mixture.
3. Process until the ice cream is ready.

PASSION FRUIT ICE CREAM

1 recipe vanilla ice cream (see pages **13** and **15**)
3 passion fruits

1. Make the vanilla ice cream per the instructions.
2. Scoop out the passion fruit and stir it into the ice cream mixture. Pour the mixture through a sieve to strain out any fruit pits, if desired.
3. Process until the ice cream is ready.

BROWN SUGAR ICE CREAM

1 recipe vanilla ice cream, omitting granulated sugar (see pages **13** and **15**)
6 tablespoons brown sugar

1. Make the vanilla ice cream per the instructions, but substitute the brown sugar for the granulated sugar.
2. Process until the ice cream is ready.

EXTRA-RICH CHOCOLATE ICE CREAM

It was this ice cream that convinced me to make my own ice cream at home—and I even made it without an ice cream machine. The Kahlúa can be omitted or another liqueur substituted, but including the liqueur will make the ice cream softer and prevent any ice crystals from forming.

MAKES 1 PINT

1¼ cups heavy cream
2 tablespoons cocoa
3½ oz. chopped dark chocolate (70% cacao)
1 tablespoon Kahlúa (coffee liqueur)
3 large egg yolks
⅔ cup milk
¼ cup granulated sugar
pinch of salt

1. Heat half of the heavy cream (just over ½ cup) with the cocoa in a saucepan. Use a hand whisk to help dissolve the cocoa. Heat just to the boiling point.
2. Remove the pan from the heat, add the chopped chocolate, and stir until the chocolate has melted. Pour the chocolate mixture into a bowl and stir in the rest of the cream and the Kahlúa. Place a sieve over the bowl and set it aside.
3. Lightly beat the egg yolks in a small bowl.
4. Heat the milk, sugar, and salt in a saucepan until the mixture reaches the boiling point. Slowly pour the milk mixture into the egg yolks, whisking constantly. Pour the egg/milk mixture back into the saucepan and heat, stirring constantly, until the mixture thickens. Strain it through the sieve into the chocolate mixture and stir.
5. Cover the bowl with plastic wrap and refrigerate the mixture until it is completely cold, preferably overnight. You can also place the bowl in the freezer for a while to speed up the cooling.
6. Process the chilled mixture in an ice cream machine until ready. Pour the ice cream into a chilled bowl and freeze 2–3 hours before serving.

QUICK CHOCOLATE ICE CREAM

As the name implies, this ice cream is quick and easy without losing a smidgeon of flavor or texture.

MAKES 1 PINT

⅓ cup cocoa
6 tablespoons granulated sugar
¾ cup milk
¾ cup heavy cream
1 tablespoon Kahlúa (coffee liqueur) or Baileys Irish Cream liqueur (optional)

1. Mix the cocoa and sugar together in a bowl. Pour in the milk and stir until the sugar has dissolved. Stir in the cream and, if desired, the Kahlúa or Baileys.
2. Process the mixture in the ice cream machine until ready and then pour it into a chilled bowl. Freeze 2–3 hours before serving.

EXTRAS FOR CHOCOLATE ICE CREAM

You can easily vary the previous two basic recipes for chocolate ice cream. Here are a few suggestions for the Extra-Rich Chocolate or the Quick Chocolate Ice Cream.

ROCKY ROAD ICE CREAM

1 recipe chocolate ice cream (see recipes on page **19**)
1³/₄ oz. chopped pecans
1³/₄ oz. miniature marshmallows

1. Make the ice cream per the instructions.
2. Add the chopped pecans and miniature marshmallows when the ice cream has finished processing in the machine.

CHOCOLATE RASPBERRY ICE CREAM

1 recipe chocolate ice cream (see recipes on page **19**)
3¹/₂ oz. raspberries

1. Make the ice cream per the instructions.
2. Mash the raspberries and stir them in, or add whole raspberries, when the ice cream has almost finished processing in the machine.

SPICY CHOCOLATE AND CINNAMON ICE CREAM

1 recipe chocolate ice cream (see recipes on page **19**)
1 teaspoon ground cinnamon
few pinches (to taste) of cayenne pepper

1. Make the ice cream per the instructions.
2. Add the cinnamon and cayenne pepper and process in the machine until the ice cream is ready.

STRAWBERRY ICE CREAM

This is the world's best strawberry ice cream, at least according to my friend Rasmus. He was very surprised when I told him that it had only four ingredients. Of course, you can substitute raspberries, blueberries, or any berry that is in season for the strawberries if you prefer.

MAKES 1 QUART

8³/₄ oz. strawberries
1 tablespoon fresh lemon juice
1 can sweetened condensed milk (about 14 oz.)
1 cup heavy whipping cream

1. Rinse the strawberries. Cut them into small pieces and blend to a puree with the lemon juice. Blend the puree with the condensed milk.
2. Whip the cream until fluffy and mix it into the puree. Refrigerate the mixture until it is completely cold.
3. Process the mixture in the ice cream machine until ready. Pour the ice cream into a chilled bowl and freeze.

PEACH ICE CREAM

I seldom buy fruit just to eat—strange but true—but when I am planning my next batch of ice cream, I always come home with all sorts of fresh options. Peaches are one fruit I am crazy about but rarely buy. This recipe will surely change that habit.

MAKES 1 PINT

8³/₄ oz. fresh peaches with skins on and pits removed (3-4 peaches)
3 tablespoons honey
¹/₂ teaspoon vanilla powder
2 medium eggs
¹/₄ cup granulated sugar
²/₃ cup milk
³/₄ cup heavy cream

1. Cut the peaches into small pieces and put them in a saucepan with the honey and vanilla powder. Lightly mash the peaches and simmer until soft, about 5-10 minutes. Let them cool and then blend them to a smooth puree.
2. Beat the eggs and sugar until light and fluffy.
3. Heat the milk in a saucepan to the boiling point. Slowly pour the hot milk into the egg mixture, whisking constantly. Pour the milk/egg mixture back into the saucepan and heat, stirring constantly, until the mixture thickens.
4. Pour the cream into a bowl and place a sieve over the bowl. Strain the milk/egg mixture through the sieve and blend it with the cream. Stir in the peach puree. Refrigerate the mixture until it is completely cold.
5. Process the mixture in the ice cream machine until ready. Pour the ice cream into a chilled bowl and freeze.

CHERRY ICE CREAM WITH TOASTED ALMONDS AND WHITE CHOCOLATE

Cherries and toasted almonds make up one of my favorite flavor combinations. Adding white chocolate is even better—if that's possible.

MAKES 1 PINT

1³/₄ oz. peeled and blanched almonds
7 oz. sweet cherries, with pits removed
2 tablespoons water
¹/₃ cup granulated sugar
1¹/₄ cups heavy cream
²/₃ cup milk
1 teaspoon vanilla extract
2 tablespoons cherry liqueur
1³/₄ oz. white chocolate

1. Heat the oven to 350°F. Spread the almonds on a baking sheet and toast them 10–15 minutes or until lightly browned. Let the almonds cool and then coarsely chop them. Put the almonds in a bowl and refrigerate.
2. Slice each cherry in half and combine them in a saucepan with the water and sugar. Bring to a boil and simmer 10–15 minutes or until the cherries are soft. Cool the cherries and then blend them to a puree.
3. Mix the cherry puree with the cream, milk, vanilla extract, and liqueur. Refrigerate the mixture until it is completely cold.
4. Melt the white chocolate in a double boiler or microwave.
5. Process the ice cream mixture in a machine until it's almost ready. Drizzle the white chocolate into the ice cream in a very thin stream. Stir in the almonds. Pour the ice cream into a chilled bowl and freeze.

CURRANT ICE CREAM

In my neighborhood I often pass by gardens with currant bushes covered with berries. Some people don't know what to do with their bounty—but currants are perfect for ice cream. If currants are not in season, try gooseberries or other small, fleshy berries.

MAKES 1 PINT

8³/₄ oz. red currants (fresh or frozen)
¹/₂–²/₃ cup granulated sugar (to taste)
1 tablespoon water
³/₄ cup heavy whipping cream
6 tablespoons Turkish or Greek yogurt
1 teaspoon vanilla extract

1. Mix the currants with the sugar and water in a saucepan and bring to a boil. Simmer for a few minutes or until the sugar has dissolved. Let cool.
2. Blend the currant mixture to a puree and press it through a sieve to remove the seeds.
3. Whip the cream until it has thickened slightly. Stir in the yogurt, vanilla extract, and currant puree. Refrigerate the mixture until it is completely cold.
4. Process the mixture in the ice cream machine until ready. Pour the ice cream into a chilled bowl and freeze.

BLUEBERRY ICE CREAM

During the late summer every year, it is the right of every Swede to pick wild blueberries. An amazing number of blueberries grow near where I live, and I have my secret spots for gathering them. Baking with blueberries is a great way to use your bounty, but their pure flavor is most intense in ice cream.

MAKES 1 PINT

7 oz. blueberries
6 tablespoons granulated sugar
2 tablespoons water
$1/2$ teaspoon vanilla powder
6 tablespoons milk
$2/3$ cup heavy cream

1. Mix the blueberries, sugar, water, and vanilla powder in a saucepan. Bring to a boil and simmer for 5 minutes. Cool the mixture slightly and then blend it in a food processor. Mix the blueberry puree with the milk and cream. Refrigerate the mixture until it is completely cold.
2. Process the mixture in the ice cream machine until ready. Pour the ice cream into a chilled bowl and freeze.

LEMON ICE CREAM

This recipe yields an exceptionally lovely and refreshing ice cream with a rich lemon flavor.

MAKES 1 PINT

$1/2$ tablespoon finely grated lemon peel
  (from 1 organic lemon)
6 tablespoons fresh lemon juice (about 2 lemons)
$3/4$ cup heavy cream
2 large egg yolks
$3/4$ cup milk
6 tablespoons granulated sugar

1. Put the lemon zest, lemon juice, and cream in a bowl and place a sieve over the bowl.
2. Lightly beat the egg yolks. Heat the milk and sugar in a saucepan to the boiling point. Slowly pour the hot milk mixture into the egg yolks, whisking constantly. Pour the milk/egg mixture back into the saucepan and heat, stirring constantly, until the mixture thickens. Strain the mixture through the sieve and stir it into the cream. Refrigerate the mixture until it is completely cold.
3. Process the mixture in the ice cream machine until ready. Pour the ice cream into a chilled bowl and freeze.

Raspberry Cheesecake Ice Cream (page 30), Blueberry Ice Cream (above), and Lemon Ice Cream (above)

RHUBARB ICE CREAM WITH CRUMBLE TOPPING

Rhubarb grows in many gardens, but often people don't know what to do with it all. Crumble-topped pies are good, but rhubarb ice cream topped with crumble is even better.

MAKES 2$^1\!/_2$ CUPS

CRUMBLE

$^1\!/_3$ cup all-purpose flour (or flour of choice)
2 tablespoons granulated sugar
2$^1\!/_2$ tablespoons butter

RHUBARB ICE CREAM

7 oz. rhubarb stalks
2$^1\!/_2$ tablespoons butter
$^1\!/_2$ teaspoon vanilla powder
$^1\!/_4$ cup light brown sugar
$^1\!/_4$ cup granulated sugar
pinch of salt
$^3\!/_4$ cup heavy cream
$^2\!/_3$ cup milk

PREPARING THE CRUMBLE TOPPING:

Heat the oven to 400°F. Mix all the ingredients for the crumble together, spread the mixture out on a baking sheet covered with baking parchment, and bake 8–10 minutes. Let the topping cool, then put it in a bowl and refrigerate.

MAKING THE ICE CREAM:

1. Cut the rhubarb into $^1\!/_4$–$^1\!/_2$ inch pieces. Mix the rhubarb, butter, vanilla powder, brown and granulated sugars, and salt in a saucepan and simmer until the rhubarb is soft. Cool the mixture and then blend it to a puree. If you want, set aside 3 tablespoons of the puree to drizzle over the ice cream for serving.
2. Mix the larger portion of puree with the cream and milk. Refrigerate the mixture until it is completely cold.
3. Process the mixture in the ice cream machine until ready. Layer the finished ice cream with the crumble in a bowl and drizzle it with the reserved puree. Freeze.

RASPBERRY CHEESE-CAKE ICE CREAM

MAKES 3 CUPS

8$^3\!/_4$ oz. raspberries
2–4 tablespoons plus 6 tablespoons granulated sugar (to taste)
juice from $^1\!/_2$ lemon
7 oz. cream cheese
$^3\!/_4$ cup milk
$^3\!/_8$ cup heavy cream
1$^3\!/_4$ oz. crushed digestive biscuits or graham crackers

1. Put the raspberries, the 2–4 tablespoons sugar, and the lemon juice in a saucepan and bring to a boil. Stir until the berries are soft and the sugar has dissolved, 2–3 minutes. Cool slightly, blend to a puree, and strain out the seeds. Refrigerate.
2. Beat the cream cheese and remaining sugar until creamy. Whisk in the milk and cream. Refrigerate the mixture until it is completely cold.
3. Process the cream cheese mixture and half of the raspberry puree in an ice cream machine. Layer the finished ice cream in a chilled bowl with the rest of the raspberry puree and the crushed biscuits or crackers. Freeze.

FIG AND HONEY ICE CREAM WITH MADEIRA

You can strain out the fig seeds before freezing the mixture, but I always keep them—they are beautiful and add a pleasant texture.

MAKES 1 PINT

FIGS

5 fresh figs
1/4 cup granulated sugar
2 tablespoons honey
2 tablespoons water

ICE CREAM

1 cup heavy cream
6 tablespoons milk
1/2 tablespoon Madeira wine

PREPARING THE FIGS:

Cut the stems off the figs but leave the skin on. Cut the figs into small pieces and combine them in a saucepan with the sugar, honey, and water. Bring the mixture to a boil and then simmer for 10 minutes, stirring occasionally. Let cool slightly.

MAKING THE ICE CREAM:

1. Mix the cream, milk, and Madeira wine with the fig puree. Refrigerate the mixture until it is completely cold.
2. Process the mixture in the ice cream machine until ready. Pour the ice cream into a chilled bowl and freeze.

RUM RAISIN ICE CREAM

Homemade rum raisin is a true classic.

MAKES 1 PINT

RUM RAISIN

2 2/3 oz. raisins
6 tablespoons dark rum

ICE CREAM

2 large egg yolks
2/3 cup milk
6 tablespoons granulated sugar
pinch of salt
1 cup heavy cream
2 tablespoons dark rum

PREPARING THE RUM RAISINS:

1. Combine the raisins and rum in a saucepan, bring to a boil, and simmer 2–3 minutes.
2. Pour the mixture into a bowl and let it cool for at least 2 hours.

MAKING THE ICE CREAM:

1. Lightly beat the egg yolks in a bowl.
2. Mix the milk, sugar, and salt in a saucepan and heat to the boiling point. Slowly pour the hot milk into the eggs, whisking constantly. Pour the egg/milk mixture back into the saucepan and heat, stirring constantly, until the mixture thickens.
3. Pour the cream in a bowl and place a sieve over it. Strain the egg/milk mixture into the cream. Blend it in. Stir in the rum raisins and the rum. Refrigerate until it is completely cold.
4. Process the mixture in the ice cream machine until ready. Pour the ice cream into a chilled bowl and freeze.

LICORICE ICE CREAM

Licorice is immensely popular in Sweden, so we take our licorice ice cream very seriously. I tested and revised this recipe several times before I was satisfied with the results. I tried it with licorice powder, licorice syrup, and several kinds of licorice candy, but nothing was right until I tried Kick licorice toffee. Now it is the right color. (If you don't have access to Kick, another brand of licorice toffee will do.)

MAKES 1 PINT

2 large egg yolks
$^{1}/_{4}$ cup granulated sugar
2 oz. soft licorice-flavored toffee
1 cup heavy cream
1 cup milk
licorice syrup for serving (optional)

1. Lightly beat the egg yolks and sugar together in a bowl.
2. Cut the licorice into small pieces and combine it with the cream in a saucepan. Turn the heat to medium and warm the mixture, stirring occasionally, until the licorice has melted. Slowly pour the hot licorice cream into the egg mixture, whisking constantly.
3. Pour the egg/licorice mixture into the saucepan and heat, stirring constantly, until thickened. Strain the mixture and stir it into the milk. Refrigerate the mixture until it is completely cold.
4. Process the mixture in the ice cream machine until ready. Pour the ice cream into a chilled bowl and freeze. Serve the ice cream drizzled with the licorice syrup, if desired.

PEPPERMINT ICE CREAM

A perfect creamy, peppermint-candy ice cream with a nice little crunch of the candies called "polka pigs" in Sweden. In the United States, the closest equivalent to polka pigs is old-fashioned peppermint-stick candy, but candy canes or round peppermint hard candies could be substituted.

MAKES 1 PINT

3 large egg yolks
$4^{1}/_{2}$ oz. peppermint candies
$^{3}/_{4}$ cup milk
$^{3}/_{4}$ cup heavy cream
$^{1}/_{2}$ teaspoon peppermint flavoring (optional)

1. Lightly beat the egg yolks in a bowl.
2. Heat $3^{1}/_{2}$ ounces of the peppermint candies with the milk and cream in a saucepan. Stir occasionally until the candy has melted. Slowly pour the hot milk mixture into the egg yolks, whisking constantly. Pour the mixture back into the saucepan and heat, stirring constantly, until thickened. Add the peppermint flavoring if desired. Strain the mixture and refrigerate until it is completely cold.
3. Process the mixture in the ice cream machine until ready. Pound or chop the remaining peppermint candies. Layer the ice cream and the candy in a chilled bowl and freeze.

CARAMEL ICE CREAM

Before now, you have only dreamed of ice cream this creamy and soft. Best of all, this ice cream is soft enough to scoop as soon as you take it out of the freezer. Essential when you want—or need—an immediate ice cream fix.

MAKES 1 PINT

1 cup milk
²/₃ cup heavy cream
¹/₄ teaspoon salt
²/₃ cup granulated sugar
1³/₄ oz. butter cut into cubes
3 large egg yolks
¹/₂ tablespoon dark rum

1. Pour ¹/₂ cup of the milk into a bowl and place a sieve over the bowl. Pour the rest of the milk into a saucepan and add the cream and salt. Heat the milk/cream mixture over low heat.
2. Put the sugar in another saucepan and heat on medium. Do not stir! When the sugar starts to dissolve and browns around the edges, carefully stir with a spoon from the edges toward the center so that everything melts and the sugar is completely dissolved. Stir in the butter.
3. Very carefully pour the warm milk/cream mixture into the sugar. Be careful, because the mixture may bubble up and spatter! Carefully stir the caramel mixture until it's well blended and then remove the pan from the heat.
4. Beat the egg yolks until light and airy and mix them into the warm caramel mixture. Pour this mixture back into the saucepan and heat, stirring constantly, until it has thickened. Strain the mixture into the milk that was set aside. Add the rum and stir.

Refrigerate the mixture until it is completely cold.
5. Process the mixture in the ice cream machine until ready. Pour the ice cream into a chilled bowl and freeze.

CHOCOLATE AND ORANGE ICE CREAM

Chocolate and orange are a classic combination that I've always especially liked.

MAKES 1 PINT

3¹/₂ oz. milk chocolate
1¹/₄ cups heavy cream
6 tablespoons milk
1 tablespoon finely grated orange peel
   (from 2 organic oranges)
6 tablespoons fresh orange juice
   (from 1 to 2 oranges)
¹/₄ cup granulated sugar

1. Chop the milk chocolate and put it in a bowl.
2. Heat 6 tablespoons of the heavy cream to the boiling point and then pour it over the chopped chocolate. Wait 30 seconds and then stir until the chocolate has melted. Let the chocolate cream cool and then blend in the remaining cream and the milk, orange peel, orange juice, and sugar. Refrigerate the mixture until it is completely cold.
3. Process the mixture in the ice cream machine until ready. Pour the ice cream into a chilled bowl and freeze.

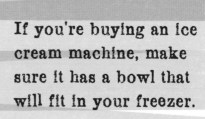

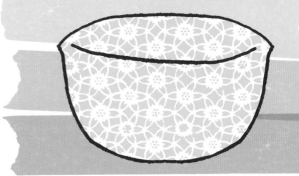

If you're buying an ice cream machine, make sure it has a bowl that will fit in your freezer.

PISTACHIO ICE CREAM

This ice cream brings out the pure flavor of the pistachios by omitting any cream. Milk has a milder flavor and allows the subtleties of the pistachio to shine.

MAKES 1 PINT

PISTACHIO CREAM

3 oz. shelled pistachio nuts
6 tablespoons warm water

ICE CREAM

1³/₄ cups milk
2 tablespoons cornstarch
6 tablespoons granulated sugar
1 teaspoon vanilla extract

PREPARING THE PISTACHIO CREAM:

Finely grind the nuts. Add the nuts and the water to a food processor and blend them until the mixture is creamy.

MAKING THE ICE CREAM:

1. Whisk together ³/₈ cup of the milk, the cornstarch, and the sugar. Pour the remaining milk into a saucepan and heat to the boiling point. Add the cornstarch mixture to the milk and simmer, stirring constantly, until the mixture has thickened, about 5–10 minutes.
2. Cool slightly and then mix in the pistachio cream and the vanilla extract. Refrigerate the mixture until it is completely cold. If you'd like, strain out any bits of pistachio nut.
3. Process the mixture in the ice cream machine until ready. Pour the ice cream into a chilled bowl and freeze.

HAZELNUT ICE CREAM

A wonderful ice cream that tastes just like Nutella. Puree the soaked hazelnuts with milk or nut milk to the desired consistency to make a nut-butter topping for the ice cream.

MAKES 1 PINT

HAZELNUTS

3¹/₂ oz. hazelnuts
¹/₃ cup granulated sugar

ICE CREAM

³/₄ cup milk
³/₄ cup heavy cream
2 tablespoons chocolate-hazelnut spread, such as Nutella
¹/₂ tablespoon hazelnut liqueur, such as Frangelico (optional)

PREPARING THE HAZELNUTS:

1. Heat the oven to 350°F. Spread the hazelnuts on a baking sheet covered with baking parchment and toast them for about 10 minutes or until golden brown. Rub the hazelnuts in a tea towel to remove their husks.
2. Blend the nuts with the sugar in a food processor until finely ground.

MAKING THE ICE CREAM:

1. Combine the ground nuts in a saucepan with the milk, cream, and chocolate-hazelnut spread and heat. Stir until the spread has melted. Cover the pan and let it stand for 30 minutes.
2. Add the Frangelico if desired. Refrigerate the mixture until it is completely cold.
3. Strain the mixture and then process it in the ice cream machine until ready. Pour the ice cream into a chilled bowl and freeze.

DULCE DE LECHE ICE CREAM WITH PECANS

When I make this recipe, I use homemade dulce de leche, which should be prepared well ahead of time, preferably a couple of days so it has plenty of time to cool thoroughly.

MAKES 1 PINT

DULCE DE LECHE

1 can dulce de leche (about 14 oz.), or homemade dulce de leche (see recipe at right)

TOASTED PECANS

1³/₄ oz. pecans
1 tablespoon butter
¹/₄ teaspoon salt

ICE CREAM

1 cup heavy cream
²/₃ cup milk
1 tablespoon dark rum

PREPARING THE TOASTED PECANS:

Heat the oven to 300°F. Spread the pecans on a baking sheet with the butter, cut into small pieces. Sprinkle the salt over the pecans. Toast the pecans in the oven 20–25 minutes, turning them occasionally. Cool and then chop the nuts.

MAKING THE ICE CREAM:

1. Mix the dulce de leche, cream, milk, and rum in a bowl. Refrigerate the mixture until it is completely cold.
2. Process the mixture in the ice cream machine until almost ready. Stir in the nuts and finish processing. Pour the ice cream into a chilled bowl and freeze.

TO MAKE DULCE DE LECHE FROM CONDENSED MILK:

Remove the paper label from a can of sweetened condensed milk, pierce two holes in the top of the can, and place it in a saucepan filled with simmering water. The water should come up to within an inch of the rim of the can. Simmer until the milk becomes a thick caramel cream, approximately 1–1¹/₂ hours. Make sure that the water level remains within one-half to one inch of the top rim the whole time—if the water bubbles too high, it could get into the can.

COCONUT ICE CREAM

These days, coconut is enjoying a surge in popularity, but it's always been one of my favorites. With toasted coconut flakes, coconut milk, and coconut liqueur, this ice cream will take the cake, so to speak.

MAKES 1 PINT

6 tablespoons coconut flakes
²/₃ cup milk
¹/₃ cup granulated sugar
³/₄ cup extra creamy coconut milk (80% coconut)
³/₄ cup heavy cream
1 tablespoon coconut liqueur, such as Malibu Rum, or 1¹/₂ tablespoons coconut liqueur extract and ¹/₂ tablespoon rum

1. Heat the oven to 350°F. Spread the coconut flakes on a baking sheet covered with baking parchment paper and lightly toast them for about 5 minutes or until light golden brown. Keep an eye on them, as they can burn easily.
2. Pour the milk into a saucepan and add the toasted coconut flakes. Heat the mixture to the boiling point. Remove the pan from the heat and put the lid on; let it stand for 30 minutes.
3. Whisk the sugar, coconut milk, and cream together. Place a sieve over the bowl. Pour the warm milk/coconut mixture into the cream mixture through the sieve to remove any coconut flakes (skip this step if you want the coconut flakes in the ice cream). Press down on the flakes to extract as much milk as possible.
4. Add the coconut liqueur, or the extract and rum, to the mixture. Refrigerate until it is completely cold.
5. Process the mixture in the ice cream machine until almost ready. Pour the ice cream into a chilled bowl and freeze.

PEANUT BUTTER AND CHOCOLATE CHIP ICE CREAM

Here's a flavor I can never get enough of. This quintessentially American combination of flavors is one of my favorite imports. Instead of chocolate chips, consider adding chopped peanut butter cups or other nut candies.

MAKES 1 PINT

1 cup milk
¹/₃ cup granulated sugar
6 tablespoons smooth peanut butter
³/₄ cup heavy cream
1¹/₂ oz. chopped roasted peanuts
1³/₄ oz. chocolate chips or chopped chocolate (light or dark, max 70% cacao)

1. Heat the milk, sugar, and peanut butter in a saucepan until the sugar and peanut butter have dissolved. Pour the cream into a bowl. Combine the warm milk/peanut butter mixture with the cream and refrigerate until it is completely cold.
2. Process the mixture in the ice cream machine until almost ready and then, at the last minute, add the chopped peanuts and chocolate chips. Pour the ice cream into a chilled bowl and freeze.

CRÈME BRÛLÉE ICE CREAM WITH MACADAMIA CRUNCH

The candied macadamia nuts make this an unbelievably decadent ice cream.

MAKES 1 PINT

MACADAMIA CRUNCH

1³/₄ oz. roasted and salted macadamia nuts
²/₃ cup granulated sugar

CRÈME BRÛLÉE ICE CREAM

³/₄ cup milk
¹/₂ teaspoon vanilla powder
¹/₄ teaspoon salt
4 large egg yolks
¹/₃ cup granulated sugar
³/₄ cup heavy cream

PREPARING THE MACADAMIA CRUNCH:

1. Chop the macadamia nuts rather finely. Cover a baking sheet with baking parchment.
2. Put the sugar in a saucepan and heat it on medium. Do not stir! When the sugar starts to dissolve and is brown around the edges, carefully stir it from the edges toward the center until the sugar has completely dissolved. Add the chopped nuts and stir quickly but carefully to avoid spattering the hot caramel.
3. Spread the caramelized nuts as evenly as possible on the baking sheet. Let set and cool 10–15 minutes. Crush or chop the nuts into smaller pieces.

MAKING THE ICE CREAM:

1. Mix the milk, vanilla powder, and salt in a saucepan and heat to the boiling point.
2. Beat the egg yolks and sugar together until very light and fluffy and then carefully pour the hot milk mixture into the eggs, whisking constantly. Pour the milk/egg mixture back into the saucepan and heat, stirring constantly, until the mixture thickens. Pour the cream into a bowl and place a sieve on the bowl. Strain the milk/egg mixture into the cream and blend. Refrigerate.
3. Process the mixture in the ice cream machine, adding the nut crunch when it is almost ready. Process the ice cream a bit more, pour it into a chilled bowl, and then freeze.

MINT ICE CREAM WITH CHOCOLATE CHIPS

Add the peppermint flavoring a few drops at a time until you have the right amount of mint flavor. Play with natural food coloring to create the classic mint green hue.

MAKES 1 PINT

1 cup milk
1 cup heavy cream
6 tablespoons granulated sugar
1–1¹/₂ teaspoons peppermint flavoring
1–2 drops green or blue natural food coloring (optional) or gel or paste food coloring
2²/₃ oz. finely chopped dark chocolate (70% cacao)

1. Combine the milk, cream, sugar, peppermint flavoring, and if desired, food coloring in a bowl and stir until the sugar dissolves.
2. Process the mixture in the ice cream machine and add the chocolate when it is almost finished. Pour the ice cream into a bowl and freeze.

DOUBLE MALTED MILK ICE CREAM

The powdered-milk mix I like to use is Nestle's Nido, which can be found in many well-stocked grocery stores with an international section. If you can't find Nido, malted milk powder is a delightful substitute. Chocolate-covered malted milk balls are usually available in the candy aisle of most grocery stores. Look for them in the bulk candy section, too.

MAKES 1 PINT

$1^{1}/_{4}$ cups heavy cream
6 tablespoons malted milk powder ($1^{3}/_{4}$ oz.)
1 teaspoon vanilla extract
2 large egg yolks
6 tablespoons milk
$^{1}/_{3}$ cup granulated sugar
pinch of salt
$3^{1}/_{2}$ oz. malted milk balls

1. Combine the cream, milk powder, and vanilla extract in a bowl and place a sieve on the bowl.
2. In another bowl, lightly beat the egg yolks. Combine the milk, sugar, and salt in a saucepan and heat to the boiling point. Slowly pour the hot milk mixture into the egg yolks, whisking constantly. Pour the milk/egg mixture back into the saucepan and heat, stirring constantly, until the mixture thickens. Strain the milk/egg mixture into the cream and blend it in. Refrigerate the mixture until it is completely cold.
3. Coarsely chop the malted milk balls. Process the mixture in the ice cream machine until ready. Layer the ice cream and the malted milk ball bits in a chilled bowl and freeze.

ORANGE ICE CREAM WITH BLACK SESAME SEEDS

Orange and sesame seeds pair well together, balancing citrus zest and earthy seeds. (Think of it as the new lemon and poppy seeds.) The texture is nontraditional but the flavor combination delivers in spades.

MAKES 1 PINT

$^{1}/_{4}$ cup black sesame seeds
$1^{1}/_{4}$ cups heavy cream
$^{3}/_{4}$ cup milk
6 tablespoons granulated sugar
grated peel from 1 organic orange
2 teaspoons orange juice

1. Toast the sesame seeds in a frying pan until they begin to release a nutty aroma.
2. Put the seeds in a blender and add $^{1}/_{4}$ cup of the cream. Blend to a smooth paste and then blend in the rest of the cream and the milk, sugar, orange zest, and orange juice. Refrigerate the mixture until it is completely cold.
3. Process the mixture in the ice cream machine until ready. Pour the ice cream into a chilled bowl and freeze.

ZABAGLIONE ICE CREAM WITH BISCOTTI

Zabaglione is an Italian dessert made by whisking together egg yolks, sugar, and usually Marsala wine into a light and airy cream. It is typically served with fresh berries, but in this case, I've paired it with another Italian classic—biscotti.

MAKES 1 PINT

3 large egg yolks
1/3 cup granulated sugar
6 tablespoons milk
pinch of salt
3/4 cup heavy cream
1/3–1/2 cup Marsala wine (to taste)
1 3/4 oz. packaged biscotti (I use almond)

1. Whisk the egg yolks and sugar together until light and fluffy.
2. Combine the milk and salt in a saucepan and heat to the boiling point. Slowly stir the hot milk into the egg yolks, whisking constantly. Pour the milk/egg mixture back into the saucepan and heat, stirring constantly, until the mixture thickens.
3. Pour the cream into a bowl and place a sieve on the bowl. Strain the milk/egg mixture into the cream and blend it in. Add the Marsala wine. Refrigerate the mixture until it is completely cold. Coarsely chop the biscotti and set them aside.
4. Process the mixture in the ice cream machine until ready. Layer the ice cream and the biscotti pieces in a chilled bowl and freeze.

Note: If you have the time and are feeling creative, you can make homemade biscotti for this recipe.

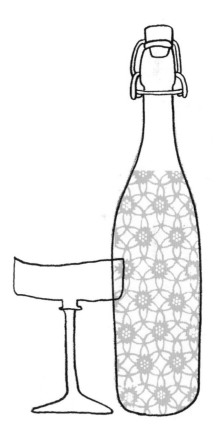

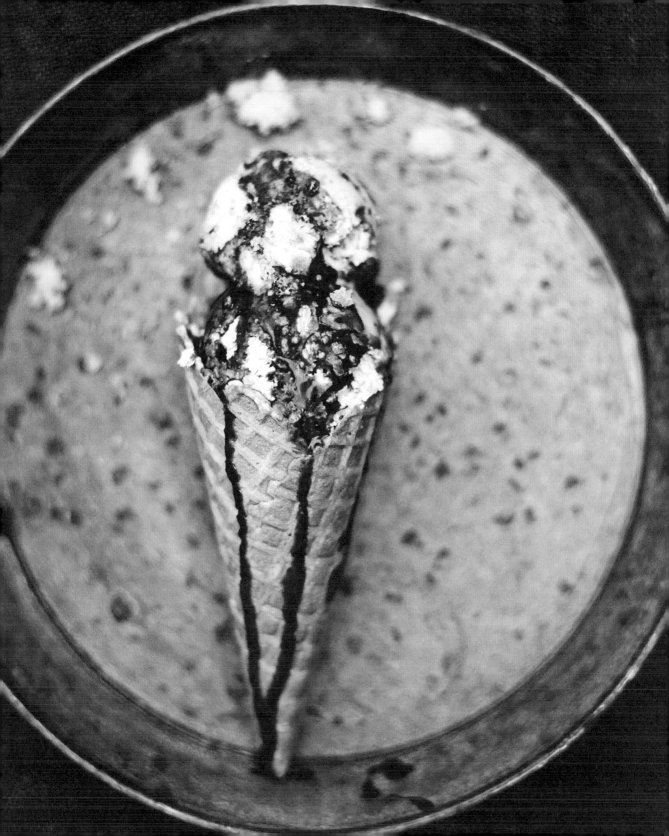

IRISH COFFEE ICE CREAM

This inventive recipe redefines Irish coffee: just add chocolate.

MAKES 1¾ CUPS

CHOCOLATE-COOKIE RIPPLE

5 chocolate sandwich cookies
3 tablespoons Baileys Irish Cream liqueur

ICE CREAM

½ cup heavy cream
2 tablespoons Baileys Irish Cream liqueur
1 large egg yolk
½ cup milk
¼ cup granulated sugar
2 teaspoons instant coffee powder
pinch of salt

PREPARING THE COOKIE RIPPLE:

1. Process the cookies in a blender to fine crumbs.
2. Add Baileys and process until thick. Pour the mixture into a bowl and refrigerate until cold.

MAKING THE ICE CREAM:

1. Pour the cream and Baileys in a bowl and put a sieve over it. In a smaller bowl, whisk the egg yolk.
2. Combine the milk, sugar, coffee powder, and salt in a saucepan and heat until its boiling point and the coffee has dissolved. Slowly pour the hot mixture into the egg yolk, whisking constantly. Return to the saucepan and heat, stirring constantly, until the mixture thickens. Strain the milk/egg mixture into the cream mixture and blend. Refrigerate to cool.
3. Process the mixture in the ice cream machine until ready. Layer the ice cream and the chocolate-cookie ripple in a chilled bowl and freeze.

TIRAMISU ICE CREAM

This ice cream doesn't get much more indulgent, with its chocolate-and-coffee ripple.

MAKES 3 CUPS

CHOCOLATE-AND-COFFEE RIPPLE

⅓ cup granulated sugar
6 tablespoons cold, strong coffee or espresso
3 tablespoons cocoa
¼ teaspoon vanilla powder

ICE CREAM

8¾ oz. mascarpone
1¾ oz. cream cheese
⅔ cup heavy cream
⅔ cup milk
pinch of salt
¼ cup granulated sugar
¼ cup Kahlúa (coffee liqueur)

TOPPING

Ladyfinger cookies or other light cookie, such as digestive biscuits or graham crackers

PREPARING THE RIPPLE:

Combine the ripple ingredients in a saucepan and simmer 3–4 minutes. Pour it into a bowl and cool slightly. Cover with plastic wrap and refrigerate until cold.

MAKING THE ICE CREAM:

1. Whisk the mascarpone and cream cheese until creamy. Add the cream, milk, salt, sugar, and Kahlúa and beat until smooth. Refrigerate until completely cold.
2. Process in the ice cream machine until ready. Layer ice cream and ripple in a chilled bowl and freeze. Serve topped with crushed ladyfinger cookies.

MAPLE SYRUP AND WALNUT ICE CREAM

I sweeten this ice cream with maple syrup instead of sugar to highlight the syrup's wonderful flavor.

MAKES 1 PINT

CANDIED WALNUTS

³/₄ cup walnuts
¹/₄ cup maple syrup

ICE CREAM

2 large egg yolks
³/₄ cup milk
pinch of salt
³/₄ cup heavy cream
6 tablespoons maple syrup
1 teaspoon vanilla extract

PREPARING THE CANDIED WALNUTS:

1. Heat the oven to 350°F. Spread walnuts on a baking sheet covered with baking parchment and toast for 10 minutes or until light golden brown. Let them cool and then chop coarsely.
2. Heat the maple syrup in a saucepan just to the boiling point. Add the nuts and remove the pan from the heat. Pour the mixture into a bowl and cool in the refrigerator.

MAKING THE ICE CREAM:

1. Lightly beat the egg yolks in a bowl. Combine the milk and salt in a saucepan and heat to the boiling point. Slowly pour the hot milk into the egg yolks, whisking constantly. Pour the milk/egg mixture back into the saucepan and heat, stirring constantly, until the mixture thickens. Pour the cream into a bowl and place a sieve over it. Strain the milk/egg mixture into the cream and blend it in. Mix in the maple syrup and vanilla extract. Refrigerate the mixture until it is completely cold.
2. Process the mixture in the ice cream machine. Add the nuts when the ice cream is almost ready. Pour it into a chilled bowl and freeze.

EARL GREY ICE CREAM

Earl Grey tea's citrusy flavor happens to be perfectly suited to ice cream.

MAKES 2¹/₂ CUPS

1¹/₄ cups milk
3 bags Earl Grey tea
6 tablespoons granulated sugar
3 large egg yolks
³/₄ cup heavy cream
1 teaspoon vanilla extract

1. Pour the milk into a saucepan and heat to the boiling point. Add the tea bags, cover, and let steep for about 10 minutes. Remove the teabags.
2. Whisk the sugar and egg yolks together. Slowly pour the hot milk into the egg mixture, whisking constantly. Pour the milk/egg mixture back into the saucepan and heat, stirring constantly, until it thickens. Pour the cream into a bowl and place a sieve over it. Strain the milk/egg mixture into the cream and blend it in. Add the vanilla extract and refrigerate the mixture until it is completely cold.
3. Process in the ice cream machine until ready. Pour into a chilled bowl and freeze.

ESPRESSO SEMIFREDDO WITH CHOCOLATE CARAMEL

This lovely, candy-like ice cream has a bold coffee flavor. Choose soft chocolate caramels for the best results.

MAKES ABOUT 1 QUART

1/3 cup espresso or strong coffee
1 tablespoon Kahlúa (coffee liqueur)
4 large egg yolks
4 large egg whites
1/2 cup granulated sugar
1 1/4 cups heavy whipping cream
3 1/2 oz. chocolate caramels, such as Rolo or Caramello
1 3/4 oz. shaved dark or milk chocolate at room temperature

1. Line a 1-quart bread pan with plastic wrap. Let the wrap hang over the edges so you can easily pull the ice cream out of the pan once it is frozen.
2. Beat the espresso or coffee, the Kahlúa, and the egg yolks in a bowl. In another bowl, whip the egg whites and sugar together to a thick meringue.
3. In a third bowl, whip the cream until firm and then add the espresso mixture. Next, fold in the meringue.
4. Chop the chocolate caramels into small pieces and stir them into the ice cream mixture. Pour the mixture into the lined pan and freeze for about 6 hours.
5. Shave the chocolate and serve the semifreddo with the chocolate on top.

BROWNED BUTTER–MAPLE SEMIFREDDO

Browned butter adds a fantastic flavor to baked goods and sweets, and ice cream is no exception. It is important to use unsalted butter to prevent salt crystals from forming in the ice cream.

MAKES ABOUT 1 QUART

2 2/3 oz. unsalted butter
1/2 cup maple syrup
4 large egg yolks
1 3/4 cups heavy whipping cream

1. Heat the butter in a saucepan until it is golden brown and acquires a nutty smell. Set it aside to cool.
2. In another saucepan, simmer the maple syrup for about 2 minutes.
3. Whisk the egg yolks until light and fluffy and then stir in the maple syrup and the browned butter. Refrigerate the mixture until it is completely cold.
4. Whip the cream until firm and then blend it into the egg mixture. Pour the ice cream mixture into a bowl and freeze 4–6 hours.

RASPBERRY SEMIFREDDO WITH TURKISH PEPPER (SALT LICORICE)

Raspberries and salt licorice are a wonderful combination that I was doubtful about at first. Now I've changed my mind and use it frequently. In Sweden, Turkish pepper is a hard, salty, slightly spicy licorice candy with a liquid center. It is a specialty food that hasn't quite made the leap across the Atlantic.

MAKES ABOUT 1 QUART

7 oz. frozen or fresh raspberries
6 tablespoons confectioners' sugar
2 teaspoons cherry liqueur
grated peel and juice from $\frac{1}{2}$ lemon
3 large egg whites
$1\frac{1}{4}$ cups heavy whipping cream
$1\frac{3}{4}$ oz. Turkish pepper (salt licorice)

1. Combine the raspberries, about 2 tablespoons of the confectioners' sugar, the cherry liqueur, and the lemon zest and juice in a saucepan. Bring to a boil and then simmer for about 5 minutes or until the berries are soft. Strain the mixture if you want to remove the seeds, and then let it cool.
2. Whip the egg whites until they begin to foam and then gradually add the rest of the confectioners' sugar.
3. Whip the cream until it's firm and then fold it into the egg-white mixture. Stir in the raspberry compote.
4. Crush the licorice in a mortar and stir it into the ice cream mixture. Pour the ice cream into a bowl and freeze 4–6 hours.

DULCE DE LECHE AND CHOCOLATE SEMIFREDDO

*This semifreddo is unbelievably good even
though it is made without an ice cream
machine. The meringue pieces are a nice little
surprise. I use homemade dulce de leche,
which should be made well ahead of time.*

MAKES ABOUT 1 QUART

DULCE DE LECHE

1 can dulce de leche (about 14 oz.), or homemade
    dulce de leche (see recipe on page **41**)

ICE CREAM

3 large egg whites
$^3/_8$ cup granulated sugar
$^3/_4$ cup heavy whipping cream
$4^1/_2$ oz. dark chocolate (70% cacao)
$2^1/_2$ tablespoons butter
about 10 Crispy Meringues ($1^3/_4$ oz., see page **101**)

MAKING THE SEMIFREDDO:

1. Whip the egg whites and sugar to firm peaks.
   In another bowl, whip the cream.
2. Melt the chocolate and butter together in a
   saucepan. Mix in $^3/_8$ cup of the dulce de leche
   and stir until the mixture is smooth. Combine
   the cooled chocolate mixture with the
   whipped cream and then fold in the egg-white
   mixture. Pour this mixture into a baking pan
   and spoon in the rest of the dulce de leche.
3. Crush the meringues and stir them into the
   ice cream mixture. Freeze the ice cream 4–6
   hours.

SORBET AND SHERBET

APRICOT SORBET

This is a fantastic and refreshing soft sorbet made with apricots and almond liqueur.

MAKES 2 $^1\!/_2$ CUPS

17 $^1\!/_2$ oz. fresh apricots with skin on (about 17 fruits)
$^2\!/_3$ cup water
$^2\!/_3$ cup granulated sugar
$^1\!/_2$–$^3\!/_4$ tablespoon amaretto (almond liqueur)

1. Slice the apricots down the center and remove the pit from each. Cut the halves into smaller pieces and combine them with the water in a saucepan. Simmer 5–10 minutes or until the fruit is soft. Add the sugar and simmer for another minute or until the sugar has dissolved. Let the mixture cool.
2. Process the apricots into a puree in a blender. Add the amaretto and refrigerate the mixture until it is completely cold.
3. Process the mixture in an ice cream machine until the sorbet is ready. Pour it into a chilled bowl and freeze.

PLUM SORBET

The type of plum you choose will affect the color and flavor of this sorbet. I prefer a dark plum to bring out an intense red color. Taste one of your plums first to make sure the plums are really ripe and sweet.

MAKES 1 PINT

17½ oz. plums with skins on (about 9 fruits)
1 tablespoon light brown sugar
juice of ½ lemon
6 tablespoons water
about ½ cup granulated sugar (to taste)
2 teaspoons vodka

1. Heat the oven to 350°F. Split the plums and remove the pits. Place the plum halves on a baking sheet and sprinkle them with the brown sugar. Bake in the oven on the center rack 30–35 minutes. Let the plums cool.
2. Mix the plums with the lemon juice, water, sugar, and vodka and process to a smooth puree in a blender. Refrigerate the mixture until it is completely cold.
3. Process the mixture in an ice cream machine until the sorbet is ready. Pour it into a chilled bowl and freeze.

KIWI SORBET

This is the perfect ice cream for anyone who loves kiwifruit. The tiny seeds add a fun texture, but you can strain them out before freezing if you prefer.

MAKES 3 CUPS

$^2/_3$ cup water
$^2/_3$ cup granulated sugar
$17^1/_2$ oz. kiwi (about 7 large fruits)
juice of $^1/_2$ lemon
2 teaspoons vodka

1. Boil the water and sugar together until the sugar dissolves. Let the syrup cool.
2. Peel and slice the kiwis, removing the hard center pit (see Tip below). Combine the fruit, sugar syrup, lemon juice, and vodka in a blender and puree until smooth. Refrigerate the mixture until it is completely cold.
3. Process the mixture in an ice cream machine until the sorbet is ready. Pour it into a chilled bowl and freeze.

STRAWBERRY AND CHAMPAGNE SORBET

Everyone knows that strawberries and champagne are a winning combination, and that holds true even when they're frozen.

MAKES 1 PINT

$^1/_4$ cup water
$^1/_4$ cup granulated sugar
9 oz. strawberries
1 tablespoon lemon juice
$^2/_3$ cup champagne or sparkling white wine

1. Boil the water and sugar together until the sugar dissolves. Let the syrup cool.
2. Rinse the strawberries and cut them into small pieces. Combine the strawberries with the sugar syrup, lemon juice, and champagne in a blender and puree until smooth. Refrigerate the mixture until it is completely cold.
3. Process the mixture in an ice cream machine until the sorbet is ready. Pour it into a chilled bowl and freeze.

Tip: An easy way to prepare kiwifruit is to slice each one lengthwise and carve out the center.

WATERMELON SORBET

This lovely sorbet is refreshing and ever so good. I recommend serving it on a hot summer day. Fun tip: Save the rind of one half of the melon in which to serve the ice cream.

MAKES 1 PINT

6 tablespoons water
6 tablespoons granulated sugar
17 1/2 oz. watermelon, sliced in half with flesh
    scooped out
juice of 1 lime

1. Boil the water and sugar together until the sugar dissolves. Let the sugar syrup cool.
2. Cut the watermelon into small pieces and remove the seeds. Combine the watermelon with the sugar syrup and lime juice in a blender and puree until it's smooth. Refrigerate the mixture until it is completely cold.
3. Process the mixture in an ice cream machine until the sorbet is ready. Pour it into a chilled bowl or scooped-out watermelon rind and freeze.

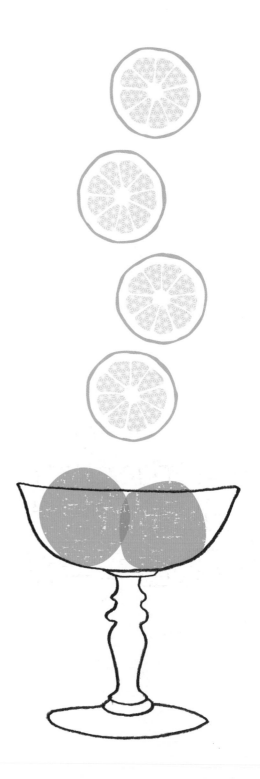

RASPBERRY SHERBET

Serve this sherbet alongside a scoop of homemade chocolate ice cream.

MAKES 1 PINT

9 oz. raspberries
1 cup milk
6 tablespoons granulated sugar
juice of $1/2$ lemon
1 teaspoon vodka

1. Combine the raspberries, milk, and sugar in a blender and puree until smooth. Strain out the seeds. Add the lemon juice and vodka to the puree and refrigerate until it is completely cold.
2. Process in an ice cream machine until ready. Pour it into a chilled bowl and freeze.

GRAPEFRUIT SORBET

This is a beautiful, refreshing sorbet that I can't get enough of.

MAKES $2^{1}/_{2}$ CUPS

$2^{1}/_{4}$ cups freshly squeezed grapefruit juice
    (3 to 4 grapefruit)
$1/2$ cup granulated sugar
1 tablespoon white wine (optional)
2 teaspoons vodka

1. Combine $3/4$ cup of the juice with the sugar in a saucepan and boil until the sugar dissolves. Add the rest of the juice, the wine, if used, and the vodka. Refrigerate until it is completely cold.
2. Process in an ice cream machine until the sorbet is ready. Pour into a chilled bowl and freeze.

CHOCOLATE AND PORTER SORBET

This ice cream has become a favorite at my house. It might seem a bit unusual to have beer in ice cream, but beer paired with chocolate is a surprisingly good combination of flavors. The malt characteristics of the beer are enhanced when combined with chocolate. Choose a porter that is not very bitter (such as Fuller's London Porter, or your favorite local option).

MAKES 1 3/4 CUPS

1/2 cup water
6 tablespoons granulated sugar
4 tablespoons cocoa
pinch of salt
2 2/3 oz. dark chocolate (70% cacao)
6 tablespoons porter or stout
1 teaspoon vanilla extract

1. Combine the water, sugar, cocoa, and salt in a saucepan and bring to a boil. Stir as the mixture simmers for 1 minute or until the cocoa has dissolved. Remove from heat.
2. Coarsely chop the chocolate. Add it to the mixture in the saucepan and heat until the chocolate has melted. Stir in the beer and vanilla extract. Refrigerate the mixture until it is completely cold.
3. Process the mixture in an ice cream machine until the sorbet is ready. Pour it into a chilled bowl and freeze.

CITRUS SORBET

A refreshing sorbet with a strong, sparkling citrus flavor.

MAKES 1 PINT

1 tablespoon grated orange peel
    (from 2 organic oranges)
6 tablespoons granulated sugar
pinch of salt
1 cup freshly squeezed citrus juice
    (from about 2 oranges and 1 lemon)
1/2 tablespoon citrus liqueur, such as Grand
    Marnier or Cointreau
2/3 cup heavy whipping cream

1. Process the orange zest, sugar, and salt in a blender. Add the citrus juices and citrus liqueur.
2. Lightly whip the cream and combine it with the other ingredients. Refrigerate the mixture until it is completely cold.
3. Process the mixture in an ice cream machine until the sorbet is ready. Pour it into a chilled bowl and freeze.

POMEGRANATE SHERBET

Instead of juicing fresh pomegranates for this sorbet, it is fine to use commercially squeezed pure pomegranate juice. You can find it in any well-stocked grocery.

MAKES 1 PINT

³/₄ cup pomegranate juice (about 2–3 pomegranates)
6 tablespoons heavy cream
6 tablespoons milk
6 tablespoons granulated sugar
juice from ¹/₂ lemon
2 teaspoons vodka

1. Combine all the ingredients and stir until the sugar is dissolved. Refrigerate the mixture until it is completely cold.
2. Process the mixture in an ice cream machine until the sherbet is ready. Pour it into a chilled bowl and freeze.

ICE CREAM POPS

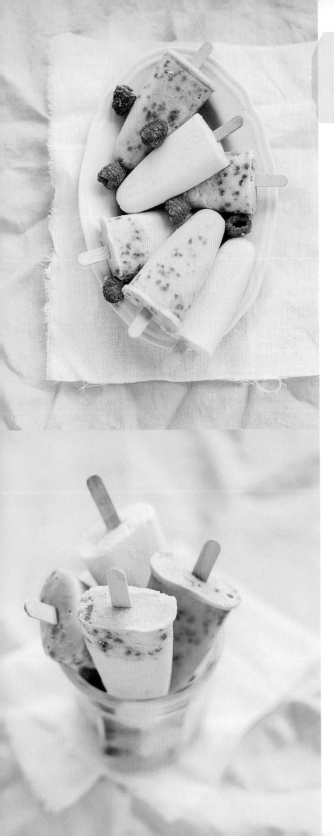

RASPBERRY AND VANILLA ICE CREAM POPS

Supereasy and tasty ice cream pops that you can pull together in no time.

MAKES 4–6 ICE CREAM POPS

1 recipe Quick Vanilla Ice Cream (see page **13**)
2²/₃ oz. raspberries

1. Make one recipe of Quick Vanilla Ice Cream but do not process it in the machine.
2. Mash the raspberries and mix them into the ice cream or put them whole into the ice cream pop molds.
3. Pour the ice cream into the molds. Freeze about 1 hour or until the ice cream has hardened somewhat. Insert the ice cream sticks and freeze another 3–4 hours.
4. Serve the ice cream pops directly from the freezer or store them in the freezer in a lidded plastic container.

BLUEBERRY AND YOGURT ICE CREAM POPS

These ice cream pops are fresh, healthy, and just sweet enough to feel like a treat.

MAKES 4–6 ICE CREAM POPS

$2^2/_3$ oz. blueberries
$^1/_8$ cup granulated sugar
1 tablespoon lemon juice
1 cup Turkish or Greek yogurt (10% fat)
2 tablespoons honey

1. Combine the blueberries, sugar, and lemon juice in a saucepan. Heat up the mixture and then simmer for 5 minutes. Let the blueberry mixture cool and then process it in a blender to a puree.
2. Mix the yogurt and honey in a bowl. Layer the yogurt mixture and blueberry puree in the ice cream pop molds. Freeze for about 1 hour or until the ice cream has hardened somewhat. Insert the ice cream sticks and freeze another 3–4 hours.
3. Serve the ice cream pops directly from the freezer or store them in the freezer in a lidded plastic container.

CHOCOLATE ICE CREAM POPS WITH PISTACHIOS

These ice cream pops are almost like eating chocolate pudding on a stick. Instead of egg yolks, cornstarch makes the ice cream really creamy and thick without the heaviness of cream.

MAKES 4–6 ICE CREAM POPS

ICE CREAM

$2^1/_2$ tablespoons cornstarch
$1^2/_3$ cups milk
$^1/_4$ cup granulated sugar
2 teaspoons cocoa
pinch of salt
$1^3/_4$ oz. chopped dark chocolate (70% cacao)

CHOCOLATE COATING

$3^1/_2$ oz. chopped chocolate
   (whatever type you like)
$^1/_4$ cup chopped pistachio nuts

MAKING THE ICE CREAM:

1. Whisk the cornstarch and $^1/_4$ cup of the milk together to make a smooth paste. Combine the rest of the milk with the sugar, cocoa, and salt in a saucepan; bring to a boil.
2. Remove the pan from the heat and whisk in the cornstarch mixture, poured in a thin stream. Put the pan back on medium heat and whisk until the mixture thickens, about 1–2 minutes. Mix in the chocolate and stir until the chocolates melts.
3. Let the mixture cool slightly before you pour it into the molds. Carefully tap the molds on the table to prevent air bubbles. Freeze about $1–1^1/_2$ hours. Insert the ice cream sticks and freeze another 3–4 hours.

4. Remove the pops from the freezer and quickly dip the molds into a glass of warm water. Carefully remove the ice cream pops from the molds and lay them on a plate covered with parchment paper. Put the plate in the freezer.

PREPARING THE CHOCOLATE COATING:

1. Melt the chocolate in a double boiler or in the microwave. Let it cool slightly. Dip the top of each ice cream pop in the chocolate or pour the chocolate over each bar and let it run over the ice cream. Dip each ice cream pop into the chopped pistachio nuts; the chocolate hardens in just a few seconds.
2. Serve the pops immediately or store them in the freezer in a lidded plastic container.

ICE CREAM CAKES AND DESSERTS

The World's Easiest Ice Cream Cake (see page 81)

BERRY ICE CREAM CAKE WITH CHOCOLATE-DIPPED CONE

I once saw a cake topped with an ice cream cone, and I never stopped thinking about how I might re-create the idea . . .

MAKES 8–10 SLICES

BERRY ICE CREAM CAKE

12¼ oz. berries (about 1½ cups)
grated peel and juice of 1 organic lemon
1 can sweetened condensed milk (about 14 oz.)
1¾ cups heavy whipping cream
¾ cup milk
1 teaspoon vanilla

TOPPING

5¼ oz. chopped dark chocolate (70% cacao)
2 oz. (½ stick) butter
sprinkles, such as nonpareil sprinkles
1 ice cream cone

MAKING THE BERRY ICE CREAM CAKE:

1. Lightly mash the berries and mix them with the grated lemon peel and lemon juice. Process the mix to a puree. Strain out the seeds if you want. Blend the puree with the condensed milk.
2. Whip the cream until soft and fluffy, then fold in the berry puree, milk, and vanilla extract.
3. Pour the mixture into a springform pan approximately 7 inches in diameter and 3½ inches high. Carefully tap the pan on the table to eliminate any air bubbles. Cover it with plastic wrap and freeze for at least 6 hours or overnight.

PREPARING THE TOPPING:

1. Slowly melt the chocolate and butter in a saucepan, then let it cool slightly.
2. Take the cake from the freezer, release it from the pan, and place it on a chilled plate.
3. Pour the chocolate over the cake (save a portion for the ice cream cone topper). Use a spoon or offset spatula to even out the chocolate and let it run down over the rim of the cake. Work fast because the chocolate hardens quickly. Using the remaining chocolate, form a small mound at the center of the cake and decorate it with sprinkles before the chocolate hardens.
4. If there is room in the freezer, place the ice cream cone upside down on the cake's chocolate mound; otherwise, freeze the cake without the cone. Remove the cake from the freezer a few minutes before serving and top it with the cone if you haven't already.

WORLD'S EASIEST ICE CREAM CAKE

You won't find a prettier, better, or easier ice cream cake than this.

MAKES 1 QUART

1 double recipe of your choice of ice cream (1 quart)
berries or chocolate shavings (optional)

1. Make the ice cream following the recipe and process it in the ice cream machine until it is half frozen. Pour the mixture into any kind of freezer-safe cake mold that holds about 1 quart. Freeze 4–6 hours before serving.
2. Remove the cake from the freezer and leave it at room temperature for about 10 minutes before setting it on a chilled plate. If desired, decorate the cake with berries, chocolate shavings, or homemade pennants.

ROCKY ROAD ICE CREAM CAKE

One of my absolutely top ice cream cake recipes, which I make again and again. Confession: Once my partner and I ate the entire cake in one day—yes, just the two of us . . . no regrets.

MAKES 8–10 SLICES

ICE CREAM

6 tablespoons cocoa
3/4 cup milk
2 1/4 cups heavy cream
1 can sweetened condensed milk (about 14 oz.)
2 teaspoons vanilla extract
1 3/4 oz. peanuts (about 6 tablespoons)
1 3/4 oz. chocolate chips and peanut butter chips
about 1 oz. minimarshmallows

COOKIE BASE

5 1/4 oz. chocolate sandwich cookies (10–11 cookies)
5 1/4 oz. digestive biscuits (10 cookies)
3 1/2 oz. melted butter

TOPPING

1/2 recipe Hot Fudge Sauce (see page **101**)
handful of peanuts
handful of chocolate and peanut butter chips
handful of minimarshmallows

MAKING THE ICE CREAM:

1. Combine the cocoa and milk in a saucepan and heat until the cocoa dissolves. Blend in the cream, condensed milk, and vanilla extract. Place the bowl in the freezer so the mixture can harden.
2. Chop the peanuts and mix them with the chocolate chips, peanut butter chips, and minimarshmallows in a bowl. Set the mixture aside.

PREPARING THE COOKIE BASE:

1. Crush the chocolate sandwich cookies and the digestive biscuits to fine crumbs (or process them in a blender). Combine the crumbs with the melted butter and press them into the bottom and up the sides of a springform pan that is 7 inches in diameter and has sides that are 3 1/2 inches high, or use a pan that holds about 1.7 quarts. Freeze 20–30 minutes.
2. After the ice cream has slightly thickened in the freezer, blend in the peanut mix and then pour the ice cream over the cookie base in the springform pan. Cover the pan with plastic wrap and freeze again, for about 6 hours or overnight.

ADDING THE TOPPING:

1. Spread the hot fudge sauce over the cake. Decorate the cake with the extra chopped peanuts, chocolate and peanut butter chips, and minimarshmallows.
2. Serve the cake right away or store it in the freezer. Don't forget to take the cake out of the freezer a couple of minutes before serving.

NEAPOLITAN ICE CREAM CAKE

This cake takes some time to prepare, but it's ever so tasty, as well as beautiful and stunning. It isn't a difficult recipe but does require several steps.

MAKES 8–10 SLICES

SANDWICH BASE

8 tablespoons (1 stick) butter at room temperature
1 cup light brown sugar
2 large eggs
1 teaspoon vanilla extract
2¼ cups all-purpose flour
6 tablespoons cocoa
1 teaspoon baking powder
¼ teaspoon salt

ICE CREAM

2¼ cups heavy cream
1 can sweetened condensed milk (about 14 oz.)
2 teaspoons vanilla extract
3½ oz. sweet cherries, with pits removed
2 tablespoons granulated sugar
juice of ½ lemon
1 tablespoon cherry liqueur
1¾ oz. pistachio nuts
natural food coloring (optional)

TOPPING

3½ oz. chopped dark chocolate (70% cacao)
2 tablespoons butter
fresh cherries
handful of chopped pistachios

PREPARING THE SANDWICH BASE:

1. Beat the butter and brown sugar until fluffy, about 2–3 minutes. Add the eggs, one at a time, as you continue beating, and then add the vanilla extract.

2. Combine the flour, cocoa, baking powder, and salt in a bowl. Sift the flour mixture and stir, a little at a time, into the egg mixture to form the dough. Cover the bowl with plastic wrap and refrigerate for at least 1 hour.

3. Heat the oven to 350°F. Cover two baking sheets with baking parchment.

4. On a floured board or counter, roll out the dough to about ⅛ inch thick. Use a pizza cutter to cut four layers. To make the ice cream cake, I use a standard loaf pan (3¼ × 10¾ inches at the base and 4¼ × 11¾ inches at the top of the pan, with sides approximately 2¾ inches high), so the individual layers should measure as follows:

   3¼ × 10½ inches
   3½ × 10¾ inches
   4 × 10⅞ inches
   4⅛ × 11¼ inches

5. Place the layers on the baking sheets and bake 8–9 minutes.

MAKING THE ICE CREAM:

1. Mix the heavy cream, condensed milk, and vanilla extract. Divide the mixture into three equal portions and refrigerate one of them.

2. Halve the cherries and remove the pits, then combine the cherries with the sugar and lemon juice in a saucepan. Simmer 5–10 minutes or until cherries are soft. Let cool.

3. Put the cherries in a blender and process to a smooth puree; blend in the cherry liqueur.

continued on next page ⟹→

Blend the cherry puree with one-third of the unrefrigerated ice cream mixture and then refrigerate.

4. Finely grind the pistachios in a blender and then fold them into the other one-third of the unrefrigerated ice cream mixture. If you like, color the mixture with a small amount of green gel or paste food coloring. Refrigerate.

ASSEMBLING THE ICE CREAM CAKE:

1. Cut two strips of baking parchment for the bottom of the pan, one narrow running the length of the pan, and the other wide, for the width of the pan, with an extra inch or two above the sides so you can use the strips to remove the cake from the pan.

2. Place the smallest layer of the sandwich cookie on the bottom of the pan. Pour in half of the refrigerated vanilla ice cream. Place the pan in the freezer for about 20 minutes so the bottom layer can harden somewhat.

3. Remove the pan from the freezer and place the second-smallest cookie layer on top. Pour in the pistachio ice cream. Freeze for about 20 minutes to harden the ice cream.

4. Lay the next-to-largest cookie layer on top and pour in the rest of the vanilla ice cream. Freeze for another 20 minutes.

5. Remove the pan from the freezer and place the largest cookie layer on top. Pour the cherry ice cream over it.

6. Cover the pan with parchment paper and freeze 4–6 hours or overnight.

PREPARING THE TOPPING:

1. Remove the ice cream cake from the freezer. After a few minutes at room temperature, use the paper strips to help lift the cake from the pan. Place the cake on a chilled platter and put it back in the freezer while you prepare the chocolate topping.

2. Slowly melt the chocolate and butter together in a saucepan. Let it cool.

3. Remove the ice cream cake from the freezer. Be prepared with an offset spatula, because once you start spreading the chocolate, it hardens quickly. Spread the chocolate over the top of the cake. Press down on the chocolate at the edges so that the topping runs down the sides. Decorate the cake with the fresh cherries and chopped pistachios. Serve the ice cream cake immediately or store it in the freezer.

FRIED BANANAS WITH ICE CREAM AND CARAMEL SAUCE

If you are really daring, you can flambé the bananas. Far more conservative, I am satisfied with just frying them, and I swear that method works just as well.

MAKES 4 SERVINGS

FRIED BANANAS

4 bananas
$2^1/_2$ tablespoons butter
$3/_8$ cup brown sugar
$1/_4$ teaspoon vanilla powder
$1/_4$ cup dark rum (optional)

FOR SERVING

1 pint ice cream; for example, vanilla (see pages **13** and **15**)
caramel or chocolate sauce (see pages **101–2**)

PREPARING THE FRIED BANANAS:

1. Peel the bananas and slice them down the center.
2. Combine the butter, sugar, vanilla powder, and rum, if used, in a large frying pan. Heat the ingredients until the butter has melted and the mixture is bubbly and has thickened slightly. Place the bananas in the pan and fry them 1–2 minutes.

SERVING THE BANANAS AND ICE CREAM:

Place the warm bananas in dishes, put ice cream on top of the bananas, and top with caramel or chocolate sauce.

ICE CREAM TART

Here's a nice and somewhat novel way to serve ice cream: atop a cookie-tart base.

MAKES 6–8 SERVINGS

COOKIE BASE

$10^1/_2$ oz. chocolate sandwich cookies (or cookies of choice)
$3^1/_2$ oz. melted butter

FILLING

$1^1/_4$ cups Chocolate-Caramel Sauce (see page **102**)
about 14 scoops (or 1 quart) of ice cream; for example, caramel, chocolate, and vanilla ice cream (see pages **13**, **15**, **19**, and **36**)
6 tablespoons Caramel Sauce with Rum (see page **102**)

PREPARING THE COOKIE-TART BASE:

Crush the cookies to fine crumbs (or process them in a blender). Mix the crumbs with the melted butter and spread the mixture over the bottom and up the sides of a tart pan. Freeze 20–30 minutes to harden.

FILLING THE TARTS:

1. Fill the tart shell with the chocolate-caramel sauce. Freeze for about 2 hours.
2. Scoop out ice cream balls and arrange them in the pie shell. Drizzle caramel sauce over the tart and serve.

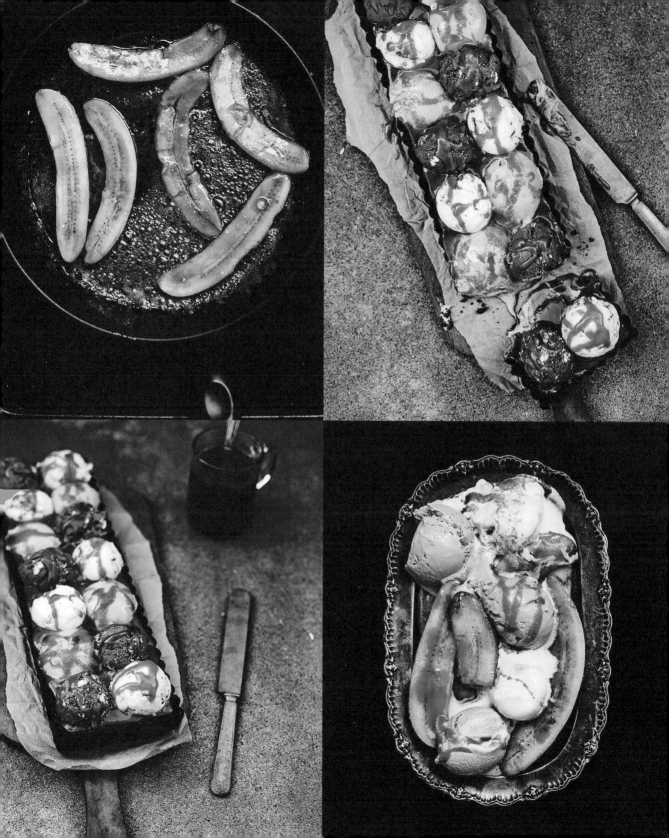

Chocolate Chip Cookie Sandwiches with Vanilla Ice Cream

BROWNIE-COOKIE SANDWICHES WITH CARAMEL ICE CREAM

Dreamy brownie-like cookies filled with the softest caramel ice cream.

MAKES ABOUT 10 WHOLE COOKIES
OR 5 ICE CREAM SANDWICHES

6 oz. dark chocolate (70% cacao)
2$\frac{1}{2}$ tablespoons butter
1 large egg
$\frac{1}{3}$ cup granulated sugar
1 teaspoon vanilla sugar
$\frac{1}{4}$ cup all-purpose flour
$\frac{1}{8}$ teaspoon baking powder
1 recipe Caramel Ice Cream (see page **36**)

1. Heat the oven to 350°F. Melt 3$\frac{1}{2}$ ounces of the chocolate with the butter in a saucepan. Combine the egg, sugar, and vanilla sugar in a bowl and beat until light and fluffy, about 8–10 minutes.
2. Chop the remaining 2$\frac{1}{2}$ ounces of chocolate. Sift the flour and baking powder in a bowl. Fold the flour mixture, the melted chocolate/butter mixture, and the chopped chocolate into the egg mixture. Let the dough rest for about 15 minutes at room temperature.
3. Scoop about 2 tablespoons of dough for each cookie onto a baking sheet covered with baking parchment. Bake the cookies 8–10 minutes.
4. Cool the cookies and then fill pairs of them with caramel ice cream. Store the ice cream sandwiches in the freezer or serve them immediately.

CHOCOLATE CHIP COOKIE SANDWICHES WITH VANILLA ICE CREAM

My favorite chocolate chip cookies with the right balance of softness and crispness, paired with vanilla ice cream.

MAKES ABOUT 10 WHOLE COOKIES
OR 5 ICE CREAM SANDWICHES

2$\frac{2}{3}$ oz. butter (about 5$\frac{1}{2}$ tablespoons)
1 cup all-purpose flour
pinch of salt
$\frac{1}{2}$ teaspoon baking soda
6 tablespoons light brown sugar
$\frac{1}{4}$ cup granulated sugar
$\frac{1}{2}$ teaspoon vanilla powder
1 large egg
2$\frac{2}{3}$ oz. dark chocolate (70% cacao) or dark chocolate chips
2$\frac{2}{3}$ oz. milk chocolate or milk chocolate chips
1 recipe vanilla ice cream (see pages **13** and **15**)

1. Melt the butter and let it cool. Sift the flour, salt, and baking soda into a bowl.
2. Combine the melted butter, the sugars, and the vanilla powder in a large bowl. Add the egg and beat. Fold in the flour mixture and the chocolate chips. Mix until the dough comes together. Cover the bowl with plastic wrap and refrigerate 1 hour.
3. Heat the oven to 325°F. Roll small balls (about 2 tablespoons) of the dough and place them well-spaced on a baking sheet covered with baking parchment. Bake 10–12 minutes. Let the cookies cool and then place them in the freezer for a while.
4. Fill pairs of cookies with the vanilla ice cream. Store them in the freezer or serve immediately.

DRINKS

AFFOGATO

In my opinion, coffee is the best drink in the world (besides water). What can make coffee better? A scoop of vanilla ice cream and a little chocolate or caramel sauce.

strong fresh-brewed coffee or espresso
vanilla ice cream (see pages **13** and **15**)
your choice of chocolate or caramel sauce
    (see pages **101**–**2**)
liqueur, such as Kahlúa (coffee liqueur),
    Baileys, or Frangelico (hazelnut liqueur)

Serve a cup of the freshly brewed coffee or espresso with 1 or 2 scoops of vanilla ice cream and layer with your choice of sauce and liqueur.

When making an ice cream float, keep in mind that the soda or carbonated soft drink will froth up and bubble over when you add ice cream.

Most commercial carbonated soft drinks have natural, classic origins. Healthier, naturally sweetened root beers are available all over, along with all sorts of other natural sodas. Try a ginger brew float, or pair a scoop of ice cream with juniper berry soda. The sky is the limit.

ICE CREAM FLOATS

Floats and ice cream sodas, as they are called in the United States, are popular drinks made with one or more scoops of ice cream and some type of sweetened soft drink. The most universal float may be made with Coca-Cola and vanilla ice cream, but you can try whatever soft drink you like. Does it remind you of childhood? If you want a float that isn't so sweet, replace one-quarter to one-third of the soft drink with sparkling water or club soda. For a lighter option, pair a sorbet with sparkling water.

ROOT BEER FLOAT

1 can of root beer or other soda (12 oz.)
1 to 2 scoops vanilla ice cream
dollop heavy cream

Pour the root beer into a tall glass. Add one or more scoops of vanilla ice cream. Top with a dollop of heavy cream.

COCA-COLA FLOAT

1 can Coca-Cola (12 oz.)
1 to 2 scoops vanilla ice cream

Pour the Coca-Cola into a tall glass. Add one or more scoops of vanilla ice cream.

BERRY FLOAT

$3/4$ cup blueberry or raspberry soda (or other fruit-flavored soft drink)
$1/4$ cup + 2 tablespoons sparkling water
1 to 2 scoops vanilla ice cream
dollop heavy cream
fresh berries (optional)

Pour the soft drink and sparkling water into a tall glass. Add one or more scoops of vanilla ice cream. Top with a dollop of heavy cream and a few fresh berries, if desired.

TOPPINGS
AND EXTRAS

CRISPY ICE CREAM CONES

I use an electric krumkake griddle (popular in Scandinavia, shown opposite, top left) to make these thin ice cream cones, but you can use an old-fashioned waffle iron or a regular waffle cone maker and a cone mold. It is important to work quickly because the waffles harden in just a few seconds.

MAKES ABOUT 10 CONES

2$^{1}/_{2}$ tablespoons unsalted butter
$^{1}/_{3}$ cup all-purpose flour
pinch of salt
1 tablespoon granulated sugar
6 tablespoons confectioners' sugar
2 large egg whites, at room temperature
1 teaspoon vanilla extract
flavorings such as grated lemon peel or
   $^{1}/_{2}$ teaspoon cardamom (optional)

1. Melt the butter in a saucepan and let it cool. Sift the flour and salt into a small bowl.
2. Combine the granulated and confectioners' sugars in a large bowl. Add the egg whites and whip by hand or with an electric mixer until the mixture thickens. Beat in the vanilla extract, flour mixture, flavorings (if used), and melted butter. Beat until the dough is smooth.
3. Heat the waffle cone maker to medium and brush the plates with a little melted butter.
4. Set out some baking parchment or a plate and a cone mold for shaping the cones. If you don't have a mold, you can shape the waffles around a small cup.
5. Scoop a heaping tablespoon of thick batter for each cone and drop it onto the center of the waffle iron. Close the griddle and bake the waffle for about 1 minute. Lay the warm waffle on the parchment paper and quickly form it into a cone around the cone mold. Be careful,

as the waffle is warm. Protect your hands with a pair of thin cotton gloves. Make sure each cone holds its shape until it has completely hardened. Cool the cones on a cooling rack.

ICE CREAM CONES WITH SPRINKLES

This is perfect for children's parties because the kids can dip their cones into chocolate and then choose toppings.

3$^{1}/_{2}$ oz. chocolate, whatever type you like
Optional: sprinkles, chopped nuts, crushed candy, or any other fine topping, about one spoonful per person
10 ice cream cones, purchased or homemade

Melt the chocolate in a deep pan and let it cool until it thickens. Pour each topping into its own bowl. Dip the cones in the chocolate and then in the chosen topping. Set each cone in a glass or jar until the chocolate has hardened.

BRITTLE CRUMBLE

Add this crunchy delight to any flavor of ice cream, but it it particularly good with vanilla.

MAKES ABOUT $^{3}/_{4}$ CUP OR 4 SERVINGS

$^{2}/_{3}$ cup all-purpose flour
$^{1}/_{4}$ cup granulated sugar
1$^{3}/_{4}$ oz. (about 3$^{1}/_{2}$ tablespoons) butter

Heat the oven to 400°F. Mix all the ingredients together with a fork, or use your fingers. Spread the crumble on a baking sheet covered with baking parchment and bake 8–10 minutes. Let it cool. Serve atop your ice cream of choice.

CRISPY MERINGUES

MAKES 20–30 MERINGUES

1¾ oz. egg whites (about 3 egg whites)
6 tablespoons granulated sugar
⅔ cup confectioners' sugar
½ tablespoon lemon juice
few drops of gel or paste food coloring

1. Heat the oven to 200°F. Beat the egg whites in a clean, dry bowl. When they begin to foam, add the granulated sugar, a little at a time. Beat to a thick, white meringue. You should be able to turn the bowl quickly upside down and back without the meringue's falling out. Sift the confectioners' sugar over the meringue and carefully fold it in with a spatula. Add the lemon juice and coloring if you like.
2. Scoop out or pipe the meringues (about 1 to 1½ inches in diameter) onto a baking sheet covered with baking parchment. Bake 50–70 minutes, depending on the size of the meringues, or until they release from the parchment paper, sliding off easily.

CHEWY MERINGUES

MAKES 20–30 MERINGUES

1¾ oz. egg whites (about 3 egg whites)
¾ cup granulated sugar
flavoring such as vanilla powder or grated lemon peel (optional)
few drops of gel or paste food coloring (optional)

1. Heat oven to 200°F. Beat the egg whites with half of the sugar to stiff peaks. Whisk in the rest of the sugar and any flavoring and coloring you like.
2. Scoop out or pipe the meringues (about 2 inches in diameter) onto a baking sheet covered with baking parchment. Bake about 1 hour or until the meringues slide off the parchment paper.

EASY CHOCOLATE AND COFFEE SAUCE

This is my easiest and best recipe for chocolate sauce. If you prefer, substitute water for the coffee.

MAKES 4 SERVINGS

⅔ cup granulated sugar
¾ cup cold strong coffee or espresso
6 tablespoons cocoa
½ teaspoon vanilla powder

Combine all the ingredients in a saucepan and bring to a boil. Simmer 3–4 minutes. Pour into a bowl and let cool.

HOT FUDGE SAUCE

Here's a fantastic chocolate sauce made with dark chocolate. You can serve it warm or at room temperature.

MAKES ABOUT 4 SERVINGS

⅜ cup heavy cream
⅓ cup granulated sugar
1 tablespoon golden syrup or natural corn syrup
1¾ oz. chopped dark chocolate (70% cacao)
2½ tablespoons butter

Combine the cream, sugar, and syrup in a saucepan and bring to a simmer. Remove the pan from the heat and add the chocolate and butter. Stir until everything has melted. Serve immediately or let the syrup cool slightly.

CHOCOLATE-CARAMEL SAUCE

Like the Hot Fudge Sauce, this sauce can be served warm or at room temperature.

MAKES 6–8 SERVINGS

1 can sweetened condensed milk (about 14 oz.)
1³/₄ oz. chopped milk chocolate
1³/₄ oz. chopped dark chocolate (70% cacao)
²/₃ cup heavy cream

Combine all the ingredients in a saucepan and heat until the chocolate has melted. Pour the sauce into a bowl. Serve immediately or let it cool slightly.

CARAMEL SAUCE WITH RUM

Caramel? Rum? Say no more. But if you would prefer a nonboozy caramel sauce, substitute an equal amount of milk for the rum and it will be just as good.

MAKES 6–8 SERVINGS

¹/₄ cup rum
¹/₃ cup milk
6 tablespoons heavy cream
²/₃ cup granulated sugar
2¹/₂ tablespoons butter, diced

1. Combine the rum, milk, and cream in a sauce-pan and slowly heat on low.
2. Put the sugar in another saucepan and heat on medium. Do not stir! Heat until the sugar is golden brown, making sure it doesn't burn.
3. Add the butter and then the warm rum/cream mixture very carefully—the sauce can bubble up quickly. Stir carefully until the mixture is well blended.

4. Serve immediately or let the sauce cool slightly.

CHERRY SAUCE

This sauce is perfect when served with vanilla ice cream and toasted almonds.

MAKES 4 SERVINGS

10¹/₂ oz. sweet cherries, with pits removed
²/₃ cup cherry liqueur
¹/₃ cup granulated sugar
1 tablespoon lemon juice

Combine all the ingredients in a saucepan and boil about 25 minutes. Strain out the whole cherries but save them to serve with vanilla ice cream. Pour the sauce into a clean bowl and store it in the refrigerator.

THANKS TO:

My wonderful family!

Christian, because I fed you several bowls of ice cream a day and you never complained, not even once. You are fantastic!

Emma, unfortunately there isn't any bacon ice cream, although you wanted it so much. Thanks for all your input and help!

Patricia and Rickard, because you are always supportive.

The girls at 413—you're the best!

Roost Books
An imprint of Shambhala Publications, Inc.
Horticultural Hall
300 Massachusetts Avenue
Boston, Massachusetts 02115
roostbooks.com

Original text and photos © 2013 Linda Lomelino
English translation © 2015 Shambhala Publications, Inc.
Photography by Linda Lomelino
Designed by Katy Kimbell
Illustrations by Katy Kimbell
First published by Bonnier Fakta, Stockholm, Sweden
Published in the English language by arrangement
with Bonnier Group Agency, Stockholm, Sweden
English translation: Carol Huebscher Rhoades

9 8 7 6 5 4 3 2 1

First Edition
Printed in China

⊗This edition is printed on acid-free paper that meets the
American National Standards Institute Z39.48 Standard.
♻Shambhala Publications makes every effort to print on recycled paper.
For more information please visit www.shambhala.com.

Distributed in the United States by Penguin Random House LLC
and in Canada by Random House of Canada Ltd

Library of Congress Cataloging-in-Publication Data

Lomelino, Linda.
[Lomelinos glass. English]
Lomelino's ice cream: 79 ice creams, sorbets, and frozen treats
to make any day sweet / Linda Lomelino.
pages   cm
Originally published in Swedish under the title Lomelinos glass.
Includes index.
ISBN 978-1-61180-175-0 (alk. paper)
1. Ice cream, ices, etc. I. Title.
TX795.L75513 2015
641.86'2—dc23
2014019573

ABOUT THE AUTHOR

Linda Lomelino is a baker extraordinaire and the author of *Lomelino's Cakes* (Roost Books 2014). Having studied photography, English, and cinematography, she now runs her own company, Call Me Cupcake, where she combines her passions for baking and food photography. In her leisure time she plays bass in a band. She lives in Halmstad, Sweden. www.call-me-cupcake.blogspot.com